Rich Murphy chronicles…the shift towards a dystopia that such cornerstones of modern capitalism as inequality, driven consumerism, & a reliance on credit & technology are inexorably edging us towards. "Human value sells on the magazine rack / beside the checkout counter," he writes. This is a book of warnings, an all-seeing eye casting its gaze out into the future & outlining its potential shape based on what is happening now & will continue to happen if we do little to stop it. There is nothing gentle in its messages: "The bill for rights comes due soon." *The Left Behind* recounts a search for a nation's soul & conscience that proves fruitless, a frightening look at what surrounds us. It is a collection for, of, & about our times, but its very presence is a powerful reminder that we are not necessarily powerless to affect change.
—Mark Young, Editor, *Otoliths*

In his new collection, *The Left Behind*, Rich Murphy maneuvers time and space to bring us to a new sense of being. There are collisions in these pieces, making the conscience of these poems active and resigned. A small moment expands into the myriad consolations of a creative life. With wit, mournful logic, and the shivery creation of a new literary world, he draws us inevitably to these poems in joyful celebrations of language and the human imagination. Sheer intelligent joy runs through this book, hurray!
—Geoffrey Gatza, author of *APOLLO* and *The Albatross Around the Neck of Albert Ross*

Given his sincere and profound concern with the way all the "Main Street workers jitterbug / into suicidal face-time depressions," the poet encourages us not only to pay attention to how we have been evolving as a species but also to re-examine the kind of life we have been living. A beautiful book particularly worth reading in this trying time!
—Yuan Changming, Chief Editor, POETRY PACIFIC

Rich Murphy is an observer of the American experience. This is poetry as witness, in the vein of Emerson's "transparent eyeball" and Whitman's poet-journalist, a voice compelling both in its levelheadedness and in its wholeheartedness. At once poetical and empirical, both in conception and in its deposition, this is real-world verse with the force of parable – and the punch of recognition.
—Gregory Vincent St. Thomasino, Poetry Editor, *Eratio*

The Left Behind

The Left Behind

RICH MURPHY

THE POETRY PRESS OF PRESS AMERICANA

LOS ANGELES | HOLLYWOOD

Published by
The Poetry Press of Press Americana
at americanpopularculture.com

Cover photo by Kevin Jones, "Urban Decay in Detroit"
https://www.flickr.com/people/18519136@N00
https://creativecommons.org/licenses/by/2.0/deed.en

Library of Congress Cataloging-in-Publication Data

Names: Murphy, Rich, 1950- author.
Title: The left behind / Rich Murphy.
Description: Los Angeles : The Poetry Press of Press Americana, [2021] | Summary: "The Left Behind is a collection of poetry in conversation with the writings of Yuval Noah Harari, Daniel Dennett, Wendy Brown, Shoshana Zuboff, Keith Gessen, Ann Case, Angus Deaton, Ernest Becker, and Stephen Hawking. These poems urge humanity to think about the effects of wealth inequality, genetics, politics, capitalism, and other social issues with global impact"-- Provided by publisher.
Identifiers: LCCN 2021008014 | ISBN 9781735360126 (paperback)
Subjects: LCGFT: Poetry.
Classification: LCC PS3613.U7534 L54 2021 | DDC 811/.6--dc23
LC record available at https://lccn.loc.gov/2021008014

For Kathleen Adams

In memory of George Starbuck
who has my eternal gratitude:

IHaveNoTimeFor
BanterSirIAmAn
AncientMariner
MyShipWentDown

TABLE OF CONTENTS

THE LEFT BEHIND

[I]n experimental art, men are given the exact specifications of coming violence to their own psyches from their own counter-irritants or technology.

– Marshall McLuhan

Man is literally split in two: has an awareness of his own splendid uniqueness in that he sticks out of nature with a towering majesty, and yet he goes back into the ground a few feet in order to blindly and dumbly rot and disappear forever.

– Ernest Becker

Once such superhumans appear, there will be significant political problems with unimproved humans, who won't be able to compete…Presumably, they will die out, or become unimportant. Instead, there will be a race of self-designing beings who are improving at an ever-increasing rate.

– Stephen Hawking

IMPERIAL PROTOTYPE

[W]hat we call "deaths of despair," deaths from suicide,
from drug overdose, from alcohol-related liver diseases,
are on the upswing, and each successive birth cohort looks
like they're at higher risk. There really is a decline of
the American working class in the 20th century mortality
rates for white, non-Hispanics in the U.S.
– Ann Case and Angus Deaton

The economy that governs nudges,
and the poor, the once working class,
self-selects for self-neglect:
Without alms, death
welcomes with open arms.

Where banks channel cash flow,
professionals with elbows
and shoulder butts ponder
over whether to shrink
the means-test pool
where handouts trickle
from leaky eye-duct branches.
Pushing and shoving
at the turn-off lever,
the population thins, mystifying
even the dying volunteer.

The social-engineers in suits
(whether aware or ignorant)
through hockey-masked
and shoulder-padded agents
consol for family members
next in line to step forward.

HOMO SAPIENS DREG BASIN

[In Russia] [p]eople have died, of starvation, of depression, of alcoholism and violence, and not only have they done so quietly, they have done so *willingly*. They have praised their conquerors.

– Keith Gessen

Welcome to the scapegoat pool,
the biohazard on Main Street damming up
credit that flows between banks.
The smart lifeguards abandon
in lumps on shaded chairs hazmat suits.

With no cure worth delivering,
Lysol and Clorox spike on Wall Street.

However, the swamp stagnates in poverty
and pandemic deaths, and festering
punishes for indexes and investors
attempting an escape to global culture
on higher ground where world secrets
since tribal formations remain hidden.

While an old goat god in Speedo
and goggles doesn't step forward,
who in government would bother selecting?
The gigs and popup shops with no benefits,
the precarious people without purpose fail
in the deep despair flail.

A mass grave employing earth movers
blesses enough at the call from lobbyists
and hedge fund managers who wager
on genetic engineering and AI. I. I. I.

A PUZZLED NATION

The comfort food for manly dignity
stores in eyes and delivers on lips:
Who goes there? Friend or foe?

Crouching in couched phrases,
puffing up in pillowed words,
lotioning bad news in callous tones, oops,
managers worried about nose-bleeds
and about the ruffled feathers on a boss.

Slugging down in fear at lamed lazy
and broken psyches that need
in order to resist joining that line,

the high school grad with family
can't imagine from despair to a billion dollars:
how many hours that work week?
Resentment swinging up with a fist
won't strike at the kisser or the riches.

Means-tested people look in streets
and in mirrors too much like punching bags.

At a continental divide,
the city suits finger-wag, while rural
a classroom fingers triggers;
Puzzle makers pause for the interlude,
so the jigsaw silences.

BASELINE SHIFTING

In the dump homo sapiens is the most overwhelming of all the organisms in his primary and secondary effects on the landscape.

– J.B. Jackson

For fun, crapola Americana
with a cinderblock franchise
business model poked at tall
marshland grasses or groped
at the last oak tree grove in a town.

Fast cash extraction laminated
into credit card abs after robotics
passed industrial garbage
through car windows
and spread lap dance picnic grease
on a commuter train napkins.

Precious days slid through fatter
and fatter calendars, finger food
for throwaway humans convinced
that only money laughs.

As the expressway parking lots
point toward home to a crusty loaf
in a beer bath – Ah, virtual lives—,
same-day desperate delivery Ubers
to the instant gratification demand
where addiction GIFs guilt aside.

STOMPING GROUND BYPASS

The central nervous system
with inadequate shock absorbers
rattles, crunches, and buckles
up and down the continental spinal cord
when the asphalt economy exits
a wifi clover leaf into AI country.

The Main Street workers jitterbug
into suicidal face-time depressions.
Family farm children sprout,
becoming scarecrows as vegetables
without bumper crops stall and peter out.
Chiropractor and masseuse
with backbone enough hobo-hobo
into bandanas and boot-up
government agency in hotspots.

In the un-united states, the multiple
personalities crash into each other.
The disorder racket downloads viruses
Virginia, Georgia, and Maryland
while communities skirting
the hard-drive crime scene thank
lucky stars should the coast clear.

MILITARIZED ZONE

To drive the American economy car
around the globe, the military
harvested where cotton once grew.
The black and white world remained;

so even after NYC and Detroit rooted
the migration, where poverty proved king
recruiters sacked to fill barracks
until robotics drone on and on.

The Federal Statistics Bureau can't claim
to know whether the enlisted racial divide
wound (kindly put) ever healed at fringes
for the grunts or drill sergeants.
However, cops in Hummers picked
at fresh scabs on a nation limping
down city streets in broad daylight.

Any homeless person would say
that the North had, has, and will have
to own poor children or an adult in color
or responsibility for all.
To keep the ignorance advantage,
the draft came in under doors also
without country-wide discussion
about toward where the wheels turned.

ARMORY SONG

Let us arm our people with the culture of dialogue
and encounter.

– Pope Francis

Clichés in 10 languages scream
from the margins around many fields
during a World Ward One:
"Who goes there, Mann or Maugham?"

Footnotes dig in at the page bottoms
for anthropological trackers
and the various cultural historians.
Without common rituals, dialects,
and anthems, minefields
open for archive researchers.

Enraged storytellers and poets engage
along mired lines for dialogue.
The sight bead for each artist
brings forth character development,
rhythm, and full rifled-scope color.
Divvying and sharing without ensnaring,
the game goes without hunter
when space craft commands
potlatch soldiers on a planet.

Waving at human nature with a white flag,
the POW also watches from the gun tower.
The raw material, a child in a schoolyard,
looks toward definition, toward best beings.

ART FOR PUBLIC PLACES

From the bone brow, brain frames
produce for the sensors so that, phew,
a safety net catches breath.
While armies mine in the dark,
night watchmen hold in place
each gold border around
a flimsy myth called truth.

Event after event until tint fades
and cracks beyond cleaning . . .
the folk tale and lore lure
beyond the ability for belief.
First, the artists point out
how the ballast works
on a drifting Goldie Locks planet,
and then eyes and ears wander
from wonder to death grip freedom
as baselines and paradigms sift, shift.

When truss and trim fit together
to declare the ends for the Earth,
wet paint slaps with change (till tacky)
and the woken gallery goers
under stand for a new way for life.

THE EXTINCTION SQUAD

Attacking each psyche to build
the cyborg consumer army,
advertisers carpet bombed
with market campaigns
from internet heights
while public relations firms
shelled with cranium memes.

When the I-beams buckled and collapsed
into the brain pan and purpose cratered
at nerve endings, the white flag
pleaded for solidarity in debt.

Once the trained troops miss
that customers march
when the bank orders, implants
hack to hi-jack until engineers
hot-dogging cannon balls plash
and sipping cocktail spritzers
decide among gene pools.

HOMO DEUS INFESTATION

And having raised humanity above the beastly level of survival struggles, we will now aim to upgrade humans into gods, and turn *Homo sapiens* into *Homo Deus*.

– Yuval Noah Harari

Having eaten through every home in a nation,
termites rendered into sawdust-dollar-sign piles
judge benches, filibuster podiums,
and wooded promises from presidents.

Eyes and ears bought for the Treasury,
and the symbol parasite found the minds to mind
with debt surveillance and self-police.

The Institutes for Social Justice and Democracy
hollowed into caves for echoes and torture.
Book stack resin screamed out
through window and door.

Capitol buildings blew away into capital
where human value sells on the magazine rack
beside the checkout counter: How many sold
while the cashier counts for nothing?

So that the rich avoid prison,
live longest, and give birth to geniuses,
the aphid stealth infestation commoditized.
The poor die away, a penny in a well.

FUELED FOSSIL GOODBYE

Pumping the brakes on a pandemic
and privacy too, each nation
with oligarchic hood ornament
careens toward the intersections
through the early 21 Century.

Every snowflake and gang member
with a phone-clone gives up
DNA and self-rule under house arrest.

Bracing for possible impact at any moment,
vehicles automated with razor wire,
masks, and gloves buckle up
victims to collect data in the Uber-limo.

While attempting to coordinated
each crosshair on unique roadmaps,
populations thin while conformists
find safety at first glancing sideswipe.

When trajectory and speed align,
the dutiful crowd disappears.

Rich chromosomes and "healthy" helixes
survive through the T-bone expense,
after which free radicals get picked off
as peashooter exhaust pipes exhale.

DUSTBIN DIVING FOR ANTHEMS

Filling the global dumpster with nations,
the predator kicks in every door in every city
with computer spyware and marketing apps.

Grouped within puzzle-pieced borders,
politicians sweep up whatever cartels,
banks, and corporations spill behind

and then sweep down the streets
in fear and so shoot at black boys
but brown men will do too.

Fishnet wavelength lingerie holds
for second-hand sweet dreams that fall
upon shoulders only to weigh down
and anchor for frisking or murder
by mogul magnate mobsters.

To find a country for pledges and vows
among the kaput smart phone parts,
folding chairs, and charred coffee grounds
a barrel picking veteran forages for traces.

HEART DISEASE USA

The epidemic scar tissue forming
on the monetary circulatory system
flat-lines bread, butter, and bacon
issues along with war machines
should an EMT not arrive on time.

Descending from the market indexes
through Death Valley, by-pass strategies
crawl and ventilators stall.
Cacti and bones portend for blood stream
and militant "aum" meditations.

Without relief, the kitchen table
offers up budgets to bill collectors
who arrive to repossess and seat
on sidewalks families who obey
the gold rule: "Blame yourself."

Transfusions from offshore accounts
pipe into profiteer class-proof bunkers
and beneath compounded walls
where command bases target phones.

Contagion examines with x-ray
the culture from government to ideology
for symptoms and diagnosis
and wheels in patient voters to stare
at computer and TV for screening.

Wearing stethoscopes and side arms
the street doctors elect which pill
to swallow or which ragtag
regimen to follow into extinction.

LOG-DRUMMING THROUGH HUMAN WILDERNESS

Dancing to the algorithms
pounded out from Silicon Valley,
the tribes around the world perform.
The romp around cha-cha-ching
beats from tough touch screens
what Freud geeks drummed lame.

The switch-doctor-patrons applaud
while observing from the official stands
when the pageant prances, promenades,
and rollicks but mimic in contempt
during private deals. Neuro-circuitry
responds with Dervish hypnosis
to the primitive seductions.

The obedient and useless masses
resent and then envy in traditional costume
until favor blesses with fashion
. . . and yearning again.
The token hired black sheep, empathy
fading with neglect on reservations,
always smiles for the cameras.

The redundant irrelevant
imagined communities will pay
for the shortcuts around human nature
with flesh and bones
until senses have no home.

THE DUCHAMP BYTE COLLECTIVE

The dataist artist counts on
a vision that includes paradise
for a market marksman
and an adventurous vampire.
The profit prophet calculates
all things for the internet.

Lost in the sublime after viewing,
advertisers try to point out
the algorithmic genius strokes
but envy overwhelms with zeros and ones:
Upside down urinals turn up at the agency.

While the information pins down consumers
in a frame filled with bats, sights zero-in
on plastic cards tucked in the usual places.
Medicinal gaming drowns out a sucking
sound with quick fixes for anxiety.

The brushwork could swoosh off the buttons
on dress shirts one-by-one and loosen up ties
among the miners at the financial firm.
As rosy as tomorrow promises,
the palette streams one primary color
in six-foot mahout trenches for debtors.

Adorned with thumb prints, facial recognition
software, and drop cloths, public education
and health care lose out to prison,
fast food, and homelessness shock value.
A god hologram from the big tada cloud
penalizes for poor choices.

IT SAILED THE OCEAN BLUE

Data gathering devices Columbus
digital natives who perform
traditional backward duties
while raw materials disappear.

From the telescope on a Santa Maria,
a post-democracy, post-politics emergency
state coup captured and now plays out,
promising a Hollywood ending
for techies and hedge fund investors.

Smartphone congratulators label
with targets the welcoming party on shore
who toy with ongoing raider tools.

Shaping behavior predictable,
invisible hands without Tarot decks
farm from humans future resources.
Bumper crops sprout up
generational surprises
for covert surveillance gifting
to time killers and children too.

No barn door, no back stage,
no closed loops for inwardness
for a once naïve breath-catcher.
Laundered cruelty drapes to substitute
for once held self-evident truths.

A NORTHWEST PASSAGE

Lost in the digital surround frontier
child pioneers grow to become
farmed animals for the efficient CEOs
who pass judgment on junk bonds.

Owned by private concerns
the infant terribles with no exit try to hide
from incarceration and enforced ignorance
to develop unique identities,
inner resources, and moral sensibility.

Prodded, coaxed, and assured
with inevitability rhetoric,
electronic molesters poach for behaviors,
(polkas in chains, jigs in pillories)
for predictive products and strip
from integrity, personality, and emotion.

Automated cows, bulls, steers serve
for financial futures until farmers
abandon the cattle carcasses as noncompliant
or raw material without money for rent.

NO CONSENT

Discovered beyond shelf-space shipments
deep within planetary human resources,
around-the-clock maybe-addiction
thrives for Wall Street market men.

The certainty miners, extracting the ore
and crude from dead cow hides, from plastic
credit, from vaults, count on wealth.
Nicotine, alcohol, opioids eat into family
funds to enrich hawkers up on neuro-science.

After the manufactured promises
and the dope-friendly tickling,
the tossed receipt shows off boredom
in a box until the betting begins again
maintaining the green blood-flow.

From the fish-in-a-barrel hooked on surprise
to the planted oligarch in the assurance policy,
the sugar coated kids learn from helplessness drills.

REAL MAGIC

When pushed around the world
science collects into a dust bin
and the useless products
from yesteryear disappear.

Sucking at superstition to clean house,
the new priests in white robes
and with algorithms resting on palms
sweep up cows, pigs, and black cats.
Cathedrals, temples, and mosques
whistle in the vacuum hose.

The sterile lab shines.

Without the divining rod or wish bone
country folk poke at white mice for fun
and want the farm and pews back.

On knees for the preyer reading
crystal balls in sockets focus
before a daze brings hex, spell,
or curse, and the middle finger
can't rise to the occasion.

For a class and species,
the dissected frog introduces
while the student, chased
from the hippocampus
and the caged thalamus, protests.

What remained under the top hat
the mixing wand stirred
and cut in half until "puff."

WHEELBARROW FOR PARABLE

When the Fantasy Exchange Center
functions, each area resident wheels in
a big lie heaping with disillusionment,
irony, and broken promises for recycling.
However, the complaint department
never closes; the boisterous bartering barkers
die down to a mutter and growl
that disagreements never die.

At some tripping point, cliché
and platitude succumb to desperation,
and children parade away with a seed
for planting in dreams, an innocent baseline
narrative for generations to come.

Reconceived, a panacea story-line seduces
with the only possible passage for life.
Decades, perhaps a century
without seam or seems, an oak
with peace at root and at leaf impresses.

LANDING AT THE STATE FOR EXCEPTION

Body-surfing concepts onto a beach on a sunny day,
the insightful mussel man incites:
"All conduct is economic conduct;"
"technological Trojan horse
that is the Big Other;" "Homo Deus."
The notions poison along the shoreline,
depositing opioid carcasses,
AI poverty, and genes only for 1%.
Forecasters predict "a race of self-designing beings"
to substitute for the impotent sleepers.
High tide soon arrives drowning the owned
("the wretched, the oppressed, the defeated")
and carrying sunbathing geniuses$

Brain waves wash against imagining alternatives
that might call to attention the reduction:
Human being to human cycling through the deadener,
the coma-consumer farmed in a nest for a wallet.
Foundered, the friend to flounder
and fellow homo sapiens paddles at sand,
salt, the harbor bell, enduring great pain
to create an awakening that could replace a wake.

DOSEY DOE FOLK

By the time the win-win Jujitsu dance partner
wakes to back pain and to fake-change,
the hoarding class helping-charade has moved on,
squeezing salve from the justification apparatus.
Next season the cha-cha may register for billionaires.

The Raise Hell School for foot tapping students,
who wear invisible ink targets on t-shirt backs,
believe that the choreographer after handing out
the permission slips cheers on sidelines.

Every four years another pivot professional
promises to alter or to stop, and the amateurs
trip over scripted lines stretched before each step.
After the fall, the search for spare change
begins again for the hoofer in the dark.

ATMOSPHERIC PRESSURE

Laundering cruelty, thugs
in pressed shirts and rolled up sleeves
pound, wring, scrub before lunch.
Spotless records punctuate
for corporate punishers extracting
from the naïve and the quiet loser
who swallows resentment.

When corruption baseline shifts,
paper thin alibis skirt
for bureaucratic bruisers.
Kindness reeks and bubbles
from tubs that embrace each victim red.

A line declaring innocence
stretches across a neighborhood
where clean linen hangs:

Police tape officiates – “Copy that.”

Truth tissue stands behind each sheet
where the day-to-day theft chokes.

Systemic violence shears at the hawing
and hemming at city hall
where the handicapped drop dead
one-by-one without lowering taxes.
Sirens cliché through the streets;
race pins onto morgue bodies: suicide tags.

FARMING ACQUIESCENCE

The pitchfork precision patrols
retired from performances
when a kettle-bottom drum
and desperation lit up the whole town,
prompting 100 years later
CCTV cameras and militarized
police to lurk around every corner.

Called in then to drill for gold in wallets,
hypnotists drugged with debt
workers and scarecrows
so that resentment now rocks
to and fro nowhere jobs.
The peasants sit on executive laps
emoting wooden talking points:
Boardrooms laugh at the puppet state.

Consumed by malls and social media,
lifetimes after lifetimes in tandem
digest with permission granted
but without self-control.
Insight unshared by commuters
and shoppers imprisons for life
while any will to empower
never discovered organization:
No teach ins, no affinity groups.
"Of the people, for the people,
by the people" RIP.

CONSTITUTIONAL CRISIS

The exception rules introduce
by impressing a voting booth patina
upon all government buildings.
Stencil application persuades also.

The code book makes way for genocide,
slavery, The Fat Man, the corporate fix:
Top-down crews throughout the landscape
shoot up. Plus other needs for freedom.
Wee, the forced tour preambles about
and founders upon founders.
Framed, the constituent centuries later pleads
for the ability to earn a place to live.

Seven articles with subjects and a verb
that make duty and ambling so exceptional
other country miles drool with envy.

The bill for rights comes due soon;
Who prepares to pay the price,
including taxes: 27 in Roman currency?
The exception again rules to prove.

USING KEYS INTO THE SUNSET

During the dusk arriving for writing,
before mind-reading pans for gold
and before the thought-erasure probe
slips into the bung hole,
on the horizon touch screens twinkle.

The exhausted essayist for a last time
warns with a sonnet, a metaphor,
while the innovator shrugs off
articulated inscape for the dark.

Weaning readers focus on objects
to prevent terror under feet
from entering hollow-centered daydreams,
a melodious gee- cliff for school children.

"You are what you have" need not surface
to consciousness, to tongue, or to find ears.
Gross motor fist clutches to grab
substitute for dynamic Descartes duo.

The human drains into organism
where ownership and biology
measure, cull, and order.

Talent, internal dialogue dump
into landfills; while surfing in
via the digital age, embryos
rage from Promethean wombs.

FROM AQUEOUS HUMOUR TO SMOOTHIE

Retinal reality giggles before integration
with personal background, attitude, and mood.
Sometimes the movie is paid for but missed
and paid for again, never seen.
Other times the whole Cranium
Multimedia Center has its way
with a glossy moment so that a grainy film
blots or mops into a memory.
Good luck to the next visual
and optical axis crossing! Warning;
flailing limbs or jumping trunk.

Floating on nerve endings
between the out there novation
and the interior that continues to adjust
ergonomics, the organism lives
in a novel during the writing.
A lifespan stretches so that a hologram
slumps stumped behind the user illusion
controls while looking to edit tomorrow.

For a continent, the collective lens reports
on momentum mounds on both sides
to suggest that around the blend
the fruits from ignorance again fall.

MIMESIS CREATURES IN STATUS STATES

Dressed in costumes stolen from voyeurs,
body snatching celebrities
arrive in pod limos for flashbulbs
and smart video phones.

The look-alike mentor whispers into ears
offering full-life promises for protégés
after pitching to lure eyeballs stuck to screens:

The beat from a different drummer
cheats, recorded and using loudspeakers.

Every entourage gives up alien hopes,
unique dance steps, and individual breaths
for a vicarious ghost in matching pants;
even a logo mogul follows.

The brand yew herd animal aims
to keep the predator away,
while believing with whole hide
that a random snowflake from the atmosphere
fills the organ music with special.

EXTRAS IN THE CONGREGATION

For crowds without vision and leadership,
the cunning and cruelty baseline comforts.

Practicing whistling while setting up the trap,
the schadenfreude society member
learns to smile at an early age.
In easy chairs butchers point out
the ancient ameba and the swamp
while envy and resentment chop through
redundant neighborhoods to splay useless people.

Only the prime ribs stand for opportunity,
well-connected at private schools
unless lightning strikes success
for supposed helpless livers.
Bank priests select between stock and flock
to herd for barren earth and wolves
to present to dopamine starved sheep
sheared and slapped into couches.

Appearing live on CCTV,
the inessential personnel perform to prove
personal ineptitude for the honor; when crouching
during the screening process in living rooms,
the plots thicken in competition.

CONSPIRACY THEORY ORIGIN

With purpose eliminated
and without pay days
death by despair conspires
against the industrious breadwinner
whose luck slinked out
the backdoor when cheaper
labor tore up the living room.

Programmed not to face
the once trusted owner,
the abandoned robotic limbs
on a human by corporate bosses
malfunctioned and scapegoated,
pointing a finger as though shaking a gun
at people with less.

When relief and self-respect
came in liquid or powder only,
the well-managed body foreclosed
to crawl shamed under a stone
never to begin again with desire.

MARCH 2017: “LEFT, HAD A GOOD JOB”

As masochistic cyber crybabies
arrive at 1984 Boulevard with giggles,
heels drum in the streets.

In the Western Hemisphere
brain drains either through the sieve
in the schoolroom floor or evacuates
into the ether toward less hostile atmospheres:
Canada, Portugal, New Zealand.

The elite encircle for the right answer
or left blank for janitorial duties.
Taxpayers buy time until textbook science
leverages the genome product
into classes Alpha and Epsilon.

For the unknown citizen
who must allow for a less-than IQ,
death conditioning begins with
multi-flavored soma vapor-nipples
or spray cans for the whole gang
with a guarantee for now—
community, identity, stability.

The footnote soldier, who publishes
in boot ink “arat-a-tat-tat” on foreign earth
… until wow, tat-for-tat taps
at the dance competition:
homeland security mongers
vs. homelessness record holders.

ORIENTATION DAYS 21ST CENTURY

On the trek to the bluff
the once city dwelling democrat
crosses over The River Real
on the bridge to the Organism Orchard
where science judges for fitness, for fate.

Bible thumpers almost feel at home.

Every body belongs to camp-life
during the nation state, Exception.
Even Norm sleeps in a pup tent.
Social myth gathers to a flag for leaders,
the flagged psyches lost in a country.

Limbs have scrawled and larynxes
emblazoned onto tenement,
ranch, and town house "The Human Zoo"
for parenthetical days: A zebra hopes.
Risking the common cold,
the counselors in blue
also bunk in neighborhoods
where debunking could cost
for family members.

Coaching toddlers and tweens,
older hiker and clamberer
demonstrate so that the rebel
and rogue learn not to get big ideas
or to follow dreams and wander off
where hunting rifles lurk, anticipate.

Sociopaths lay down the trial trail;
the naturalist determines for each life length.

THE CHANGING OF THE MAD

Nostalgia stands in for background and for history
where the shifting baseline deposits.
In suit and tie, the dependable wannabe
presents to camouflage with flowers and fuzz.

The most brand new drops in to hang around
as though the old neighborhood remained.
Eventually a new improved environment claims, stakes.

Each weakling takes with it to the ash heap a generation
that basks in bells and whistles to a natural world,
sifting fauna and flora into extinction a group at a time.
The left behind choose shorter leashes, and illusion.

FOG BANK THEORY

When the future rains,
the hoarders arrive with barrels
and then reign over cupped hands
that quench for a day at a time.
A coincidence in history
crowns and ignores.

Right place/right time people
umbrella stories about genius
and heroes when fluke and selfishness
punctuate and capitalize as a right.

Mistaken for fact by mud dwellers
and drenched denizens,
the dry myths rule for eras, ages
before grateful grows into gasoline bombs.

Homo Sapiens Progress reports:
The weather cycle that brings tomorrow
yesterday in a monsoon flashes to revive
ancient dreams to become
Cistern Emperor, the Drizzle King,
and not Good Fortune Distribution Center.

GULF NOTICE

The elite envy attractors pump
from working class neighborhoods
where potholes, layoffs, and empty lots
push precarious enough for floor hand
and slick derrick developers.

Favoring an offshore gold-man sack
and a money extraction rig,
rough neck ivy league crews from exurbia
drill on multiple cold seep rental units
and convenient marts for pay lode.

Core samples from hard-hat head cavities
and well logs show up in strip mall chain store
blowout sales and social mantra advertisements
that lean on corner dopamine drive-bys.

Slang slung siphoning units at the well bore
hope to pass for derelict men
at another frac-ing job for the GDP,
while evicted tenement occupants
without the National Guard arm-twisting
find that temporary part-time gigs
lead to gentrification succor.

Geologic formulation scientists
and Salvation Army team up to fund
The Bell Nipple Foundation
to distribute vouchers and soup bowls
and to suckle crude confusion.

Left with a moon pool on the sidewalk
outside, the methane platforms
without safety valve tent until a spark.

MUTATION SPECIFICATIONS

The left-behind refused to salute
the internet-for –all-things engineering
that rockets savants and slackers
into The singularity species.

Continuing to forage human nature
for individual actualizations
deserted Bedouins light on the reward
in planetary and cosmic futility.

With the boutique tribe ending slow dances
into the night for artificial intelligence,
the janitors in tattered party hats exhausted
from waving good-bye get down
to bees wax: memories and imagination.

THE SELF-LOATHING INTERCHANGE

After many, many miles purchased,
the ridiculous internal combustion
economic engine, envy and resentment,
sputters “enough, enough” to a stop.
The piston block books cooked.
The spark plugs and bank charts spot-welded.

An electronics paradigm runs between sunlight
and robots, Sapiens not included.
The engineered elite plug to charge
with humor the organic end to the bone
bags that waste time and space.

From now on, smart accidents goof up
for good to make way for genius-gene
thoroughbreds possessing money and long lives.
On the threshold for the craved few world
people die from starvation, depression,
alcoholism, and violence, and do so quietly,
willingly to praise the conquerors.

Stephen hawks: “grease monkeys die out,
and CRISPR-humans self-design a fate.”
Droning tools at the hive and under the hood
pluck at one feather at a time,
one feather at a time.

Your Prophet,
Mussolini

OGRE AUGURY

Useful for censorship,
information-filled front-loaders
empty onto a vital word:

Advertisements, public relations,
app upgrade instructions,
system reboot, reply popup,
games, trivia and big data
bury alive for Earth Movers Inc.

The educated precariat tunnels
while the final exam for helplessness
beads on the minor foreheads
from factory-fled towns:
The left-to-depth and debt in school
burrow through strange books,
gig for room and board.

Mount Hopelessness erupts into fire
and ash where the mass grave
diggers wearing headlamps dis-cover
in foot print the understanding.

An archeologist with spoons
and dental pick may touch
about the key to a crisis
or the solution for stopping
the blood-letting in cities
centuries too late.

IMMEDIATE GRATIFICATION STRATIFICATION

Foot-tapping, queues, and taking turns
vanished when fingers snapped.
Having stolen the waiting from wanting,
the magician lavished with trinkets
until wishing well dried up.
A split-second rewards with a plastic whistle.
The pennies thrown into fountains
invented for desires and for hollow concern.
The toys and tricks distracted enough
to convince the scientist
and the moralist too that nothing
with value remained within the body.

The drums in the laboratory resound:

"Regard-less!" So the dopamine
for the imperial, champagne-bubble crowd
suckles for immortality,
while mean-spirited smiles eat at hearts
and wear out spleens and livers
among the froth and blistered landscapes.
"Cut the frontal-lobe fantasy families
from the equation using long division
and the math works out:
The money-heeled homo Deus
deserve to choose among the genius genes."

SELF-LOATHING COUP

Once holed up in mountain retreats,
fright or flight phalanxes
from big data divisions
attack along facial hairlines
and species specifications.
Unfurled, the wooden wedge
and mallet flutter over AI camps.
An immobile human body calls for aid,
and pity trades for the thalamus.
Broken hearts litter
with one last brood.
Pump houses prime
to roll out Petri dish god pods.
Instinct and game wail
on different sides
as the salient majority rules and walls.
Feeling peels from bone and muscle.
Thinking lumps with an ice cream scoop.
Surplus FEMA tents
substitute for flesh and notion
where algorithms stand erect.
Canned rationale by innovation
experts intervene to install a bonanza
from banana bunches.

LIFE AT THE PHARM

The amniotic fluids in time-release tablets,
syringes, and gel caps cradle for the survivor
after mother pushes out the brat.

Vaccines, antibiotics, aspirin, and Xanax
cushion with belly fat for cramped quarters
against a threatening anxiety.

Addicted to sit-coms in Plato's cave,
the embryo doesn't sweat
at the steel collar but tee-he-teethes
while canned laughter echoes
throughout "the day."

Alien cramps and contractions
and a patronizing slap on the ass
places for the space creature.
On a rock orbiting a fireball
while whistling at breakneck speed
to gods know where, the uterine chump
monkeys with placebos,
waits without defense, a will until ill.

BODY POLITICS

The dictator sits in the genome
with a short story and a long pointer.
Skin wraps up skeletal narrative in denial:
Happy Birthday until hapless dirt day.

At the embryo launch site witnesses anticipate
with gifts, legends, hopes, and wishes.

Not long after the orbiting parents tire,
the sun puts up with weather and cosmic forces.

Will goes about the day using an index finger
to accuse various enemies hiding in the landscape:
"Bang bang drop dead," the externalist says
and jogs everyday rain or shine.
But even the evil doers outside the body
feast at the Metabolism Bistro.

Meanwhile, inside the family gene pool,
big fish chomp on small fish or vice versa
with a rhythm that tells time for bomb experts
who try to haul out water wings and the shrimp.
Who among neighbors would dare go for a swim?

When given an opportunity the tyrant
stands on organ music and tips over a domino
in a ribcage or cranium for denouement.

SACKLER PHILANTHROPY

Think of it, ye millionaires of many markets, what glory may yet be yours…convert…the rude ores of commerce into sculptured marble.

– Joseph Choate

Adding coltan to silicon chips
beneath a mortar in a caldron,
the palmacist mixes for a billion batches.
Addiction code absorbed
through eyes for dopamine
substitutes for seduction:
Scrolling screen opioid "hi."
The hacker appeal triggers
to motivate the money exchange.
Girls and guns may assist
to close the deal but cost more
in these days when actors unite.
Better to hire a graphic mainliner.
"Afflicted by lost identity,
a whole new world . . . anxiety."

Hypno-days at the hippocampus party
make for a touching scene
with glass and user illusions
busier for wasting a redundant genes life:
The game app "Kill the pain, Time"
sets up losers for the wealth creators.

For frontal lobe hope,
depression desire lifts,
and the betting on a distant carrot
begins with hair from the dog.
Wolf!

THE FUN RUN RACE

While long ago no-pain no-gain
pharma teemed to bring
to town goofy “goo-goo” glue
that held gang psyches together
and more recently artificial intell-network
dragged in clown-bots to the public square,
the brain drain gene team shortens
for the pursuit after happiness
by breeding a three-legged smile.

The sieves in sinks gurgle
that the smart refugees stay at home:
Ex-pats erase to disappear from the radar.
After all, everybody loves
to have a constitution where science
and business marry for an ending.
One long guffaw to a burnt remain
knows about the ins and outs
presented to each generation
lost within a dream too big too frail.

SNARK

Snorting a smart-phone app
and running full-tilt on caffeine,
jogged cognitive pathways
elbow woken hours into dream.

Advertisements swarm around
the assumed corpse to lay eggs
and exhume from pockets and purses.
The stench wafts through
city streets where only
the homeless suck at life.

Precious resources slip into horizons
having been mined from colonized veins
via birthing canal and cervix.

As meme days dig with dilated eyes
through decade after decade,
at a certain point-blank to un-scroll
the dollar and mirrored friend,
empty content sits at a dawn
in a chamber with a bullet.

PLACEBO PAPARAZZO

Delivered to prescribers and nonprescribers
across the nation, The Bromide Daily Press
arrives on doorsteps and smartphones,
muscle relaxers for immediate consumption.
Platitudes and cliché sound bites yawn
on spoons to feed the hustled husband and wife
each working three part-time jobs to feed a family:
Beasts beneath burdens all about town.

Printed on pillows and tickling viewers
while feathering-in extreme weather and gun violence,
each and every issue wanders through a detour
to a rose garden photo and a RX advertisement.

To keep the drowsy robotic motions activated
while placating a pretense that awareness lives,
airbrushes swoop in with pixel or ink to adjust thoughts.
The editorial bias pied-pipes the money
from the addict to the drug maker.

THE YAWN THAT SWALLOWS THE SLEEPY HOLLOW

The digital surround sound
convinces for the computer tower guards
overseeing the red carpets.
The Oscar Award winners
parade into the praise graze.
Though the mesmerized breathers dress
with spring flair for the march,
the inevitable begs on needs
for an unexpected twist or turn ahead.
Monotone brain numbing agents
double as employable desperate solutions
who live for over-compensation practices.

Reading signs from the future
where an exit for the real and genuine
promise, the symbol finder
intent on clover leaf or footpath
sniffs out the woods and deeds,
the wound and what exceeds.
Heightened senses learned
with every grudge trudge to mistrust
reassurances, pats on the back,
and the mould that fawns and gushes:
Now, now, now choreographs
away from lenses and screens.

CHARMER IN THE DELL

Out on the troll farm
wolves dressed in sheep skin
breadcrumb the turkeys.
Addicted by degrees
to pasting eyes on plate glass
and ears to headphones,
gullible friends gobble up the lies.

The believers at the computer screens
peck and scroll across
the barnyard until ideologies
chop off feathered heads.
Stuffed and basted
internet serfs shelve
for the mocking and roasting
by the "us and them" engineers.

Living in overalls
while harvesting hearts and minds
on the polarized surface,
the poultry plumpers
around the table feed
for the violence in emotion.

ELEPHANTS ON WALL STREET

Tracking tusks, behavior shapers
whisper into ears on great heads
until earning ends and poachers pile
grey mounds for thoughtless grand kids:
Detour … One Way … Cul-de-Sac.

The elephant in street clothes
waits for a bus until camouflage catches up.
Peanut shell safety nets not needed
near the dark hearted sapient hunter.

The trunk on Hind Mountain distracts
from the scrawny tree at the big top
while the flies also flee from the scene.

No memory, no consciousness, the hide
with plastic and a job runs out bare naked
at some point without wit or wealth
to where the extraction thief
peeking through and hedging, murders.

The herds and species duck behind mountain
ranges, trampling a path to farm animal
for the ivory grower with pitchfork and spouse
from the city jungle and suburban savanna.

STREET SMARTS

Act 1, Scene 1

Prologos Park

When freedom-fighter change
outsources to the billionaire,
bit-part accomplices walk through
performing a farce with a limp.
How many times does the joke
need telling to the cast before the drama
“Democracy” begins in earnest?

Outside the drive through Laundromat
for the rich the detergent degrees
and association costumes define and own
so that the vocational master loses
to a lifetime bathing in wealth.

The unoccupied bromide factory
where PR wingmen airbrush debt slavery
and empower mammoth differentials
for the corporation and government
entangled in sex under the envy spotlight.

No one should sit down in a seat,
everyone needs to march in the street
shouting “No” to oligarch, homo Deus rule.
Let resentment practice at going without,
shutting down the markets
for the mom and pops’.

Act 1 Scene 2

Road Signs

All conduct is economic conduct:
Once I was mine; now I am theirs

No Conrad Grove of Death

All virtue and worth is placed in
a man able to deny himself his own desires,
cross his own inclinations,
and purely follow what reason directs as best,
though the appetite lean the other way…

Out of the society we live in,
the society we want to live in

Reclaim the commons: Ecology, biology,
public spaces, intellectual property

Abandon privatism and seek to share
illumination with the many

It is only one step from the existentialism
of the handicapped to that of acrobats

In experimental art, people are given
the exact specifications
for coming violence to their own psyches
from their own counter-irritants or technology

Fashion something – an object or ourselves –
and drop it into the confusion,
make an offering of it, so to speak, to the life force

Society everywhere is a living myth of significance
of human life, a defiant creation of meaning

Courage of hopelessness means not renounce
hope but get rid of the false solutions

Act 1 Scene 3

Home Sapiens

The shadow troupe played at the enlightenment
in Plato Capital Theater,
and now the universal sun welcomes
for the freak and meek:

Acting out and practicing placards
written by witty hands centered
on a shared internalized utopia.
Each foil, ham, extra, and mime
searches for a way to live with authentic talents
that bring stars through stages to Homo sapiens.

NEW DELI MEDITATION

Sandwiched between synapses
and serotonin, the meat depends
on the delivery system
to move even the smallest muscle.
Lunch can go uneaten
should the bread vehicle diet,
garnish with will power
as the cook at the cutting board might.

Best for the patron who denies a mood
while playing with silverware,
salt and pepper shakers to apply
for a Maître d position when available
or better, own the snappy biochemist
wearing the special waiter shoes.

The secretion oozing at the corners
while chewing with two baby fingers
in the air may not bring about reflection
on K-9s attacking, but digesting
ligaments and fatty veins
calls for Gill Glut to consider
innocence and guilt.

A MEADOW VIEWED FROM BRAMBLES

In the computer, the sheep
organize for the Judas goat.
Mister Butt orchestrates
into the pathological corporate state:
"Shear Luck" for fiddling
by William Gates. The second piece,
"Lamb Chop" by Donald Trump
hacks at the consumers
once enticed as voters.

Arranged and conducted
by Billy the Kid, the double-crosser,
the grazing gazers mesh
between wolf teeth, addiction code cogs
for the crank at the disposable
resource machine.

Until a reserve pump sucks and slurps
at a six foot hole in the ground
the storehouses leap over firewalls
to follow dreams, never to become sweaters.

PARTY TIME USA

The Spirit of History is out walking.
– Czeslaw Milosz

Every state similarly celebrated
when the Cold War entrenchment ended.
The malicious refugee manipulations
by the Nazis and Communists
penned for good in history books.

The faithful social engineers
from the church Orthodox Capitalism
doused with free time and no self-worth
and then tossed in the match:
opioids and alcohol.
Any industrial solidarity,
unionized or otherwise,
burst into service sector entrails.
Basalt scorched through towns.
Children screamed into the streets;
parental tailings staggered behind.

Victory sucked at the climate,
the oceans, the banks:
the opportunity for a Forever
World Fair … absconded with the tax funds
to gated communities and bunkers.

Slag-populated cities empty
into landfill cemeteries.
Refrigerator boxes and tarps
house enough for survivors
while generation baselines shift
until new normal settles in for encampments.

TOPOGRAPHICAL ERA

The power magnets within blank islands
and empty continents on business maps
draw at magnates whose moral compasses
cling to childhood refrigerators.

On the puckering globe, where ownership
denies landfill, hazardous waste sites,
and sewage, history reports
on topography and atmosphere.

Tribe members, following four-legged mammals
into extinction, on the reserve barter
for a meal while snarling at the zoo keeper.

Doused in uselessness by 1000 cities
and a billion smart-phones,
a dying culture possesses no need to spark
a Northwest Passage to enlighten for moguls.

NOVELTIES

Nurtured by conversation not isolation,
writers compose now with microphones.
Abuzz on screens, quotation marks
land on noses, tickle ears,
nip at exposed napes, and escape along eye lids.
The invading army "first word, best word"
amasses on tongue tips (finger tips).
Mashed into micro-chips and SIM card,
distance flits but fits on an LCD tray.
Dropper accessed marbles roll
in sockets to cut friction more than half
so that fiction flows anywhere.
Reflection and internal dialogue,
undiscovered, call out for an audience,
an autistic author from deep in the cranium,
but the interlocutors only convulse without end.
The story lines merge onto an expressway,
teacher gangs that encircle above a continental shelf,
a million breaths that steam and disappear.

ANCIENT SCRIPT

Spray-painted on the wall,
the same old story
diagnoses and points out
the early trauma and the epilogue.
As soon as imperial impulses
reach across borders,
organs in the body begin to fail.
Minding states and moods
and maintaining internal affairs
(spleen, kidneys, lungs),
the continence for content
stretches or compresses
into cartoon or character.
Even a continent elsewhere
recognizes when aerosol tints
mask calligraphy from stencil.
The whole gang beats up weaklings
who scrounge out a living,
while back home school boards
coast from year to year, truant;
ignored infrastructure potholes.
Guts burst into the streets so,
children run to hide.

CANNED-DO CANT

The canned can-do candidates sit stacked
on an ear-aid shelter shelf in the basement
(a Moulin Rouge can-can revival
meeting for eating during darker days to come),

a choppy transistor radio hoping
while the county collapses around fears.

Human beans, American style,
with tri-color labels as evidence
and only a rusted hunting knife
to open for survivalists.
What taste misses violence garnishes.

Fifty panic states express disrepair:
assault rifle quips shared with neighbors
and teeth grinding and chattering
as the shivers replace backbones.

Instituted checks and balances
arrived at Wall Street safe but gasp
when choked with pressing questions
and voters indebted to the big house.

Foraging the unraveling to bring good
to the table, the backyard gardener
relearns that fresh troubles call
for crisp ideas, just harvested concepts,
and simmered community.

MUNITIONS MAGNANIMITY

The targets for the tolerant
came with a gun rack and delayed
viral police how-to videos:
A ticking clock mock-calm
after the lynching parties
and National Guard deployments.

When the white man judges color
overreaching and seeking
eyeball to eyeball talk,
hair shirts march through obstacle
courses to demonstrate the suffering
that justifies hatred and tests atmosphere.

Threatened with pain that safety
in identity loses to freedom,
the Caucasian inmates tidy among stock
cells and rifled neurons
in solidarity confinement.

SCAPEGOAT BOROUGH

While jetliners escape over heads,
the neighborhood waits
for the twin terrors to collapse
from excess and a trickledown theory.

Poverty and the police, engaged in crossfire,
pin down children into crippled adults.
Generation after generation survivors
on doorsteps and sidewalks pick up pieces.

By adolescence bootstraps have been sold
for rent and confidence in someday leaving
the block sours in the gutter out front.

Only first responders (and only
with backup) enter these streets.

Follow up visits from social workers
or representatives from the Second Class
Citizens Board shelter in place,
buried among office furniture.

Mean-while among smoldering tenements
and row houses baby buggies and toddlers
promise to wealth a body for easy empathy,
a scapegoat gang to justify revenge impulses,
and a place to throw both hands.

REPORT CARD

In the hopeless classes,
desperation learns
how to work hands
and how to move legs,
quickly.
Though college courses
lead to ignored thefts
for the confident traveler,
the despairing and cowed crowd,
policed into parking lots,
study at gun-point
for final exams.
Humiliated grave seekers dig deep
into ancestry and dumpsters.
The peasantry in lessons
and in spell-being
produce for cringing from afar,
for finger-wagging,
and for appreciative sighs
from elementary-schooled
trust fund spenders.
An invisible handed pick pocket
snatches before the dunce divisions
have added militancy
to the curriculum.
Certainly, the life-long, hard-knock
master program substitutes
for computing acumen.
Three chairs fly
against family and friends
upon a mean graduation.

However, once in a while,
an accurate bottle
fills with gasoline
and stops with a rag.

ALL THE RAGE FOR ORDER

Without a legible face on surroundings
and the reader without an accomplice
to knowledge, illusion, tantrum,
and surgical violence ensue.

Alone in thought, the type suggests
so that cleaner sound than the sea
memes for empathy. A clumsy harmony
echoes and the village sleeps at night.

For the planet dweller, a word
to ears travels on a tightrope
and no meaning catches in a net.
Virtuoso hellos hope for welcome mats,
thirst with bone-china ears and viola hearts,

enough to assume a pitched wail in guttural,

enough to stomp and kick around
while waiting for reply,

enough to pin shoulders and brow
and extract from improvised lips.

SPIRITS

Surviving another musty satisfaction,
desire emerges on the streets in heavy pants
and wrinkled shirt open to seduction.
A neither-here-nor-there temptation waltzes
from around the corner in a mini-skirt disguise
stolen from a Free Will wardrobe.
In broad daylight no sneakers anywhere
in sight or within earshot:
The resignation in choosing arrives.

Wonder-full, the until-the-next-anticipated-surprise-
nomad jetting a dream without destination,
the orgasmic now-wow snags onto a new wish.
Gorging a path to salvation,
the perpetual present gouges the waiting
from wanting and wanting from waiting.

Mean-while the glocals fill time
with self-inflicted wounds,
one more life-line that uncoils into a noose.

JAGGED JAW

Creative creatures in Logos Land
kicked about pig skin until every animal
deflated, found a skillet,
or got lost in extinction.

The cheerleaders and marching band
drummed out the hiding for the gladiators.
Raw raw raw! Pitch the vermin
in an ashcan ha ha ha.

Alone with soy beans, leashed guilt,
and engineered, grass-fed meat,
the vulture culture circles around a poem
for the secret way out
from a wilderness genocide:

Peck, pick, pluck for the wish tone,
a lizard gizzard from the wizard.

The building blocks snap together
and break apart along intuition.

However, Wordsworth
while suffering from no dependent clause,
feels that the lion hunt
leaned on an independent paw.

Salvaging the wild, the salvation seeker
trips over assault weapons.

MOLECULAR APPLICATION FORM

The cell mates, being and words,
negotiate and fist fight to win
a hand and a nervous system.
When a palm buckles up a pen
for a drive, when tactile fingertips
feel for identity and orientation,
movement and direction threaten
with crisis or blank horizons.

Where shape attempts expression,
the fetal cognition position
at the waking foists
upon the day black eyes
or contracts with sanity clauses.

Before the subway grate
swallows up the homeless prisoner
the domestic dispute erupts
to declare, first that a lump
in flesh equals a voice,
and then that the unexplainable
noise remains coherent
to organisms elsewhere.

CULT CREDIT

Capitalism is a purely cultic religion,
without dogma.

– Walter Benjamin

At the capital cathedral
the bishops gesture
with incense and holy water
for parishioners to congregate
at the banks on the river me.
Nuns impressed with black and white
drive by gunning engines
so that envy rises over the rood
to where in gods we trust
and resentment rulers
strike at neighbors.
After the haircut, the sheep
celebrate for the mass chop:
Dominus vobiscum.
Gargoyles buttress for success
by scaring the poor away.
The sacristy gambles on investments
going unnoticed among vestments.
Knaves with two invisible hands eke
through green tablets in walls
to taketh from pews and giveth
to the vaults and sanctuary.
The excommunicated worship
on knees with paper cups
along the sidewalk on the Appian Way
where the sold bipeds roam.

SWITCHYARD FLASH ON 20TH CENTURY LIMITED

Only computer hard drives
prompt for species members
to remember consciousness
decoupling from information.

The train that rocked and rolled
for thought loved through tunnels
and over mountains
since memory mimed.
The challenge to the cranium,
coal car to steam puff,
for the human freight
alerted enough to empower enough
so dancers improvised.

Then the engineer, calling all cars,
leaned on an encyclopedia
unaware that track could memorize
every comma in nursery rhymes,
and television screens winked
back at the viewers not yet on a couch.

Asleep at the switch to cyborgs,
the conductor pretended to collect tickets
when in the nursing home for sapiens.

Had space craft among sentient animals
been prized among the chain gang
into a future, John Henry would have joined
in a journey, a conga line celebration.

EPILOGUE

Once I was mine; now I am theirs.

– Shoshana Zuboff

The fact is that men cannot and do not stand on their own powers. Moral dependence is a natural motive of the human condition and has to be absolved from something beyond oneself.

– Ernest Becker

VEGETATION SALAD DRESSING

Meditation breathes to dodge the coursing
flotsam and jetsam sense stimuli
that threatens and entices nerve endings
with nail chewing and lip biting.

Lashed and lidded mouths between the brow
and cheek feed on the present, the presented.

A gluttonous frontal-lobe bellies up to desire and devours.
Just above the chin an orifice merely needs.

Pond pondering stagnates on Saturn in deep space.

The hunger for a deserted island so that a notion
laps around two feet and no thought consumes.

Setting the table for the word "mum" and aum,
loose-fitting clothes and a pillow for the rump
spoon-feed for the cranium that swallows nothing
with "mmmmmmmmmmmmmmmmmmmmmm."

THE CONNOISSEUR

The marrow sucking business
requires to a certain degree.
In the field for filling up on being
a temperature due to blood flow,
but often without fever, courses,
carrying a curious interest, a temperament.

Pressing lips into a kiss formation
upon the outside world, cheeks
draw to build facial tissues with sup.
The inhalation slurps and sops
to savor and swallow what might
could supplement the limitations
in senses and imagination.

Birds whistle in conversation
with winds open to harmonics
and the "patron" letting go.
Books perch on fingertips
and flutter before the eyes
that digest for dreams and tomorrow.

Full-time with no vacations
the corpuscular nature in flesh
currents in tubes, canals, tunnels
where ligaments stretch
into violin bows, harp strings
upon spine and skeleton.

Retirement for the vacuuming nose
and living intake valve leans
against a horizon, granite

with a name and dates.
When the last smooch from home
ravens time and space
in all the seductive charms
and plays on a clarinet or flute
one last time, a note loves.

ODOR INDUSTRY

At the olfactory plants
no ancient workers show up
to the potted emitters
to sour production
among garden machinery.
Only bees busy on route
around terracotta and soil.
Repetitive trudge in drudgery
pounds into concrete and curbstone,
exhausted in another world.

As though in church,
the newer organs facing hues
first inhale to acknowledge
blossoms before sighing in euphoria.
Grandmother eyes fill
for the lungs in memory:
Rose rose into a pose.

Those angels on knees
who beg the question go to heaven
while manufacturing perfume
from manure and greenery.
At the end to a day best buddies
leave behind lily, violet, and daisy
for aromas in kitchens.
By the end for the weak
the schnoz, proboscis, or snout
hound from the foul habit
that prevents inspiring at all.

SMARTY PANTS

The window to the soul coordinates smart
for mates who weeded out lust and lies
from the garden remains.

At first the troubadours tumbled from horses
onto mandolins and cities in the West
hurried out to buy glass panes for organ pouches.

Each viewer found that falling
from hormonal heights into coffee grounds,
the lover awakens to pragmatic routines
that demand attention.

The chirp and buzz from kitchen appliances
teach while secreting glands taunt.

The passion that dissipates
into an oxytocin memory
also drools over fantasies
and drips into weekend hobbies.

Just as just, the synchronized
limping team from yesteryear
looks from two classroom pupils.

The perverse behavior
between science and capitalism
when meeting in the crowded streets
pokes out eyes: After waiting
an epoch, humans see.

SWEET TALK DAGGER

Honey dripped into the ear,
while today slits between
ribs in the back, gives rise to squirm
and applause from animals
who imagine watching.

The seduction relaxes
for the intercourse divide:
Yesterday and tomorrow.

An oracle whispers
that lecture and resentment
mark off operation
“goodbye sibling limbs.”

When one class beads
sweat and death
from the struggling caste,
decency porn climaxes.

The world spins as usual.

The rollover and cigarette
for assassin and now
smaller supporting cast, after burial
and services, aid in the forgetting.

MIRTH DAY PARITY

Each year in the cranium the hippocampus
remembers to celebrate the prefrontal cortex
off campus with cake, candles,
and last minute iced screams.

The neighborhood may swell
for eye popping and the life for the flesh
meeting current events outside,
but the hum-drum headquarters
spreads about wet blankets for the picnic
and provides for emergencies including
buckets filled with cold water.

While the genome snubs and dismisses
the later developments of the body
during life-long pulsating instincts,
the brainstem area almost never forgets.
The elephant trunk reaches
for the spinal cord in nursing homes
across America: Integrity or bust.

Amygdala and Cerebellum
may arrive early to the gala but do so
with skull and cross bones
to entertain for chromosomes
while setting up the party game
"The Adjustment Bureau or Genes."

O, the DNA landlord thumbs the scales
and a fishy feeling surfaces
for pores and follicles upon all body parts.

But when the pituitary gland prize
presents for guess who, medical glove
udder/chicken balloons explode at once
and the glucocorticoids lounge in pleasure.

<THE TRUTH>

As though on a Sunday spin
on a back country road
or humming a lullaby for toddlers
before the tuck-in,
the wedge driven between
performance and story
protects against self-infliction.
Suicide machines in display cases
remain locked for now and now:
"Do not break glass … ever."
A little hammer hangs
from a bolted chain.

Best for the behaviorist
who lacks a degree in honesty
to stick a thumb between lips
and suck at personality tests.

Nursery rhymes and fairy tales
creep up on the monster running
around on two legs but over millennia
maybe and not last week.
In the workshop "Shimmy
Shimmy Stake," where the audience
members swing mallets for fun,
the hippocampus and amygdala
never bump into each other.

Across the crowded room,
where brain function patches
together for evolution,
the human becoming
relies on all the good faith
that each buster can muster.

WORD AND DEED

In the relay between experience and story
the baton memes for the whole event
even if footnotes abound.
A tale passes off a false memory to feet,
torso, head, a reckless abandonment
exposing races to the error in ways.

The disheveled neurons
and misfiring synapses (not to mention
muscle cramps and pulled ligaments)
confuse all about the storage trunk
that runs on enmity and empathy.
Handcuffed to the chain-letter “I,”
the police cheat slips on a habit
and kneels at an altar: A confessional
provides for an emergency exit.

The pot boiler bores over
with routine logs to put out any fires,
but Prank and Sons practice at tai chi
in DNA, avoiding any headlines.
(And the mental illness
parties on in the host.)
Justice, the airbag, drives
so wee, the passenger, holds on
to the wheel to dare life.

PILLOWS AMONG TALL ORDERS

Resting heads on soft morality,
the sleepwalkers go-about decisions
deep in mud and blood on a clear day.
Lion teeth provide for lollipop kids
before jaws drop for witnesses.

Human DNA gnaws on tamers.
The undead rifle through coffin-sized
steamer trunks for the sunny side.
Curbstones, ethics, crack open
for the chicken farmer.

So that even murder screws
on a silencer before declared,
tongues seduce and suck at hard candy.
A slurp wipes out a village
and the evening news show
for pet lovers and how to buy
the latest collars for fleas.

Cognitive short-cuts with peak-end rule
wait at the bus stop for singularities
and then a solidarity and not a mob.

THE BEST IN THE WEST

Every day at the Best Western Nursing Home a mammoth gold spoon, heaped in a desperate culture (not yogurt), shatters the windows and waits for an opening in each head on a pillow. If a gullet swallows, another day dies in the short parade for living. Store rooms empty with wheelchairs, walkers, medications (television, radio, internet, liquor, sex, marijuana, and taking a drive), mops line up for convenience for any zombie metabolizing the gruel without success. Digestive gases turn up lips, making fools from anyone with eyes half-open in the area.

Wrestling aside the caretaker, who hustles the artificial sun toward clenched teeth, exhausts the restless mind moving from a bed with creative hours ahead. The slop in the gilded bowl stains clothing reminding the wearer throughout the day where the lying seems to pay off and where solitude remains the best western hotel.

PLANET EARTH HOTEL

Two unknown parties reserve room at the Planet Earth Hotel on behalf of the fellow traveler. Upon arrival the baggage is always a carryon of live leather and at check-in the clerk welcomes with a slap on the spanking new back side and the bellhop swaddles for one more mother. So the floors are elevated for the needs of the package.

When feet measure height and distance from nipples for the suckling, the moveable suite needs no carriage, no shoulders for sitting. Clearing a greater and greater space for living, the lean McMansion with legs leans and toddles, runs, and pedals round the grounds and parking lot who watches vicariously.

Whether enamored by the diving board or door-man exhaustion, the hold-over and over begins to own space to avoid boredom and kingdom come. The travel agent may promise a moon boutique vacation, but Mars Inn and Golf Club and Jupiter Ski Lodge look inviting; a career as an astronaut seems reasonable. Eventually, in the evenings the rooftop garden is scope enough and place.

Pulling the conventional adult from the hat in the lobby bar, takes a corkscrewed security team and mystery guest: Ta-da another night saved. With the Olympic-sized pool, workout center, fine dining restaurant, and the blonde sitting on a stool, childhood is the go-to for the day-by-day guest and weeks-long resident: Do not disturb written all over the aura around domestic-tourist and foreigner alike with no room for a green resort.

As the stay ticks away along the pillow seams and mattress, the room for the visit needed to continue to lengthened, but now much later (toward the weak end) the berth for girth expands also, a bulging steamer trunk. While waiting for the shuttle to the airport upgrade, the squatter suffers the rack rate for the always latest checkout when a house keeping employee arrives with a feather duster and air freshener.

THE TIME TABLE FOR KITCHENS

After the Civil War, to eliminate magnifying classes, a nation left all classes at home every day. Horn-rimmed, wire-rimmed, rimless, and Coke bottle lenses collected dust in the one place people didn't trip over furniture whether cheap imitation or handcrafted and polished cherry. Such attention to detail when dealing with bone china, crystal flutes, and beer mugs was thought to be wise by anyone with eyes.

When citizens and friends bumped into each other in the streets, "hello" was exchanged for "excuse me." In many ways each sense went blurry. Some people thought they were almost wealthy, and others thought they were almost poor. Needless to observe, the way of life became vexing with neighbors appearing in caves and with public events becoming spectacles for all to see. However, governors and tour guides assisted the astonished and belligerent and bought normalcy for the public places.

The day of the great lesson approached, and no one saw how the professor of history and the professor of science could clash. In the lecture hall the widgets fidgeted to screw faces into focus and the bankers lounged (with interest so why shouldn't they). When the dynamic duo announced that due to the course of events classes (even at houses, tenement, and hovels), were no longer a concern to those who counted and who counted all the time.

It was pointed out, “A new species would make extinct most of the audience and make others great slaves.” Antiquated, useless, and quiet the redundant tools sat on chairs, expecting next shovels and chains, after the parents of the new species exited the hall to the foyer where the flutes played bubbly music in congratulation of a more prosperous future.

AUGURY CHORD

Play it for the dog that got no master.
– Bob Dylan

Laying the ground work for the next obsession,
the prophet from a flighty attitude sprinkles
out from concave and convex shakers.

Imitation mirrors and lenses distribute for possibility,
ignoring the current byways and national parks
that merge to blur without distinction.

From here on the gibberish lines in the poem
may provoke so that the reader gives up
saving glimpses for another day.
Revisit again and again, please old friend.

Literature lovers may turn toward the earth
in a spring and propagate for all eventual lacunae.

With the suspension rigging, symbols, and duct tape
space craft astronauts hoist to meet between the ledges
whenever interregnum cleaves with all CAPS ice caps.

The Bering Strait, the Grand Canyon, a synapse
exist for rope ladders . . . as Odysseus breathed
between Scylla and Charybdis. Let's go!

WHAT WANT WANTS, WHAT NEED NEEDS

Embedded in DNA,
want manipulates in word and deed,
questioning while attending
the environmental school
that instructs where
and when to mourn.

Taught by surroundings,
the blatant kneeling
(the bowed head, the averted eyes)
that trumps genetic trickery
knows before giving voice to need.

Orienting to baseline fret
on planet limited before the urge
for behind-the-scene maneuvers,
the rest-assured disarm
and timing vices deactivate.

Each evolved hominid
without excess anxiety
treasures for now
found in the necessary.

THE LEDGE-ABLE CONSTITUTION

The hope dope hangs
on each moment.
White knuckled fingernails
dig into contingency to hold on
for a foothold in history
or for a hand from the future.
All the while,
where extinction promises
and slavery threatens,
the frown turned upside
down tears at the cliff face.
A gloat note laughter roars
from the Gorge Century
where the poor get picked from teeth.
Bald eagle and bearded vulture
peck at and mess with the grip.
An albatross tugs at the neck.
The mope goat on look out
for a few founders falls in love
with a Mead forecast.
Marx or the brothers dally where?
Swallowing cries
and saving energy for palms
that take root at a lip,
being won't accept a grip slip.

TABLE MANNER

Ensnared in the meaning web,
where stories find agreement,
the fly waits for the spider to finish eating
and return to the periphery, a harpist.
Last epoch a green headed beetle
left red welts on flesh and then
sat glued to the Western menu:
The heavens opened with all the strings
only to close with timpani sympathy.
Between understandings the murderer and thief
pluck on the dream catcher wires chord
to put to sleep with lull and “bye.”
However, swooning enough, a flighty
would-be parasite in bliss and swimming
in affirmations and re-enforcement
soon dances upon threads bare that seem cables
if not a ballroom floor – show buzz.
Eventually, the old croon choreography
gums up the variations on themes
and the winged and music stop.
Bibbed and humming the famished sits down.

PIPE DREAM CURL

From inner ear to the tactile sense that soles make,
the balance-beam dreamer among unending
changes in everything rides.

The courageous all-around clothing-filler smiles
on roiling illusions until wipeout or ripple onto sand
or drowns in the heightened anxiety and boredom
for frozen frames and shark teeth.

Land lubber lapping at ice cream,
audience members without a torso or heart
need not envy or resent.
Motion pictures without viewers now and now.

Hopscotch or roller skates prop for a start
and at least a second try at chance exhilaration.

Once off wet blanket excuses, bingo paddles,
turns, and feels for the lift a moment can lend:
That kisser lives for the lips on a planet
reeling in awe for one wet smack.

A FAILED UNITED STATE

Could it be that we are much more like
the Russians than we're ready to admit?
– Ivan Krastev

A third-world country crouches
behind Hollywood, Silicon Valley,
and the military industrial complex.
Defensive postures begin at home
where swat teams soldier and drill
around suspected hoods for show.
Psychologists and screenwriters
work at B-rated coping mechanisms.

The working stiff neighbors couch
toxic anxiety in serial TV dialogues
and minor home maintenance projects.

Oligarch gangs hire out statehood thugs
in suits to shakedown cities and towns.
Before passing along to the top,
the graft garnered and skimmed
adds up enough to harbor off shore
futures, should need be.

Each bit player knew to respond to cues
and then to perform on debt due dates
until the Covid fire revealed in 20/20:

Two chambers pumping out poverty,
while a house infested with termites
and successive resident village idiots
distract the wolf for thieves dressed
in Romulus and Remus costumes.

CULTURE CUSTODIANS

Who knows how many poets
gather at the cave mouth to change
the light for once fellow prisoners?
The news from a sun brings along
three dimensions, color,
and a horizon rotation that totes now.

An usher army with flashlights
offers to guide the yoked-to-shadows
out to the sublime in practice,
but the jeers threaten from pitch below.

Wobbling upon dictionaries
and history books on a table top,
verse voices twist and shout
while shoulder and eye sockets pop.

A midnight interregnum stretches
until a new mood metaphor moons:
a bat flattened on a granite wall.

B-FLAT IN ANVILLE

Waiting for the hammer to break,
the consolation poet leans on a broom.
The citizens from Anville read little,
busy day and night hunching backs in-sync
for the next blow from the muscle-armed
Wall Street gang members.
The ring about the ear lobes deafens
should chime chums pull out canal corks.

Dried oak consciences and steely nerves
pound on the only workbench
a robber baron ever cared to use.
Meeting exploitation with a dignified
hide that faces hard work,
the shop block community never buckles
but belches when each need arises.

Any ready resentment complained
about by the neatly molded mallet
comes from only the deepest blues
from a tempered red heat
after the longest work week
or when the owner or CEO
flies off the handle on a trip
to cheaper labor or lays off.

Grip lost to justice and parts
unknown, scattered to parts unknown,
silent bells celebrate until one day
greed again metes out a crime scene.
Without clappers the janitor sweeps
through language journaling as a witness
for archeologists … perhaps.

CULTIVATE ONE'S OWN GARDEN

During the now planetary
forever war on nature,
militarized curiosity
and the PR campaign, Innovation,
champion for comfort:
The enemy moves . . . until hammered.
Checkpoint Charlie guns down
everything dear in headlights.
An easy-chair converts into a pocket,
corrupts into a coma,
collapses into a cemetery plot.

Drawn up centuries ago, battle lines
and corporate models close off
negotiating a live-and-let-live future.
Even sister Jill jacks into the genome
to beat the odds into submission.
If not a dog, cat, corn ear, or rose,
species suffer at the gamer-gamble on survival.
A billion refugees crowd into surrounding
nations to escape glacial fossil-fueled melting.
A billion lone bodies left behind.

Hong Kong gongs (08/24/19)
to roll from sleep and into the streets.
Home-sweet-home regime change
reverberates around the world.

SCOOPING OUT THE INTERIOR

The industrial mind-farming
in – say – Iowa (the breadbasket)
and Boston (the Athens) petered out
when the drought started in the 70s.

Abandoned and wrinkling cowhands,
lacking important pointers
while instructing a homegrown tomorrow,
baked in the austerity fertilizer
made from chemical plants
for secret R&D and weapons factories.

Tax money for wars and for a rich man
project flowed and flows
freely for freedom-sacrifice,
a long fast food and big pharma holiday.

Cheating the homeland
to seed a now dirty word,
(Enlightenment) rounds up brains
for the US, where squashes, cabbage heads,
and Sleepy Hollow rot on the veins.

ACKNOWLEDGMENTS

BLAZEVOX: "Immediate Gratification Stratification," "From Aqueous Humour to Smoothie," "The Fun Run Race," "Imperial Prototype," and "Farming Acquiescence"

CARCINOGENIC POETRY: "The Failed United State"

E.RATIO: "Body Politics" and "Smarty Pants"

FORMER PEOPLE: "Augury Chord," "Armory Song" and "Art for Public Places"

LIFE AND LEGENDS: "Molecular Application Form"

WORLD LITERATURE TODAY: "Atmospheric Pressure" and "The Yawn that Swallows the Sleepy Hollow"

MARSH HAWK REVIEW: "Word and Deed"

NEW TEXAS: "Ogre Augury," "Extras in the Congregation," and "Cult Credit"

OTOLITHS: "Constitutional Crisis"

POETRY PACIFIC: "Ancient Script" and "At the Pharma"

PROJECTED LETTERS: "Scapegoat Borough," "Wheelbarrow for Parable," "New Deli Meditation," and "Munitions Magnanimity"

QUTUB MINAR REVIEW: "Real Magic"

RED SAVINA REVIEW: "The Connoisseur" and "Table Manner"

REVIEW AMERICANA: “Party Time USA,” “Dosey Doe Folk,” “Street Smarts,” and “Culture Custodians”

REVUE POS: “A Meadow Viewed from Brambles”

TERROR HOUSE MAGAZINE: “The Extinction Squad,” “Switchyard Flash on 20th Century Limited,” “Report Card,” “The Ledge-able Constitution,” and “Log-Drumming through Human Wilderness”

AUTHOR BIOGRAPHY

Rich Murphy's poetry collections have won the The Poetry Prize at Press Americana twice for *Americana* (2013) and *The Left Behind* (2020) and Gival Press Poetry Prize for *Voyeur* (2008). Books *Prophet Voice Now*, essays by Common Ground Research Network and *Practitioner Joy*, poetry by Wipf and Stock were published in 2020. He has published eight other poetry collections. He has taught at colleges and universities and is currently guest lecturer at Massachusetts College of Art and Design.

www.ingramcontent.com/pod-product-compliance
Ingram Content Group UK Ltd.
Pitfield, Milton Keynes, MK11 3LW, UK
UKHW041641190726
13854UKWH00006B/2626